Italian Maiolica

John Scott-Taggart

Cavaliere Ufficiale del Ordine al Merito della Repubblica Italiana

COUNTRY LIFE COLLECTORS' GUIDES

Foreword

This book is an introduction to Italian maiolica of the Renaissance. The choice of illustrations has been a difficult task and preference has, in general, been accorded to unpublished pieces of the finest quality from private collections.

The ownership given in the captions may change. Attributions and dating are, in default of signatures and dates, matters of opinion. 'VA' followed by a number is the number in the Victoria and Albert Museum Catalogue. The Bak sale was at Sotheby's on 7th December 1965. The letter 'A' followed by a number indicates the catalogue number of the Adda Collection described in *Islamic Pottery and Italian Maiolica* by Bernard Rackham. When the word 'dated' followed by a year is used it means the date is on the piece.

Excellent public collections of maiolica may be seen: in London (Victoria and Albert Museum, Wallace Collection, British Museum, Gambier-Parry Collection in the Courtauld Institute Gallery); in Oxford (Ashmolean Museum); in Cambridge (Fitzwilliam Museum). Abroad there are fine museum collections: in Paris (the Louvre, Cluny Museum, Petit Palais, Sèvres); in Lyon; in Florence (Bargello); in Faenza (International Museum of Ceramics); in Rotterdam (Boymans-Beuningen Museum); in New York (Metropolitan Museum). The present author's *Bibliography of Italian Maiolica* gives 3,000 references to museums, books, articles, private collections, sales in all countries from 1850 onwards. It may be consulted in the library of the Victoria and Albert Museum; all the leading museums have copies of it.

The following books will be most helpful to those seeking further information:

Bernard Rackham

Guide to Italian Maiolica. Victoria and Albert Museum, 1933. (Out of print.)

Catalogue of Italian Maiolica in the Victoria and Albert Museum, 1940. (Vol. 2 – Illustrations. Out of print.)

Italian Maiolica. Faber & Faber, 2nd ed. 1964.

Islamic Pottery and Italian Maiolica. Faber & Faber, 1959. (A detailed catalogue of the Adda Collection.)

Giuseppe Liverani

La Maiolica Italiana, 1958. (English translation: *Five Centuries of Italian Maiolica*, McGraw-Hill Book Co. Inc., 1960.)

Jeanne Giacomotti

La Majolique de la Renaissance. Paris, 1961.

G. Ballardini

Corpus della Maiolica italiana. Dated pieces to 1535. (Out of print.)

J. Chompret

Répertoire de la majolique italienne. Paris, 1949. (Out of print.)

Students of Italian maiolica owe an immense debt to the scholarship of the late Bernard Rackham, C.B., and the present writer owes him a more personal debt for his generous counsel and guidance over a period of eleven years.　　　John Scott-Taggart

Orvieto. Jug in green and manganese-brown, decorated with pinecone mouldings and a stag. Height 6 in (15·24 cm). About 1420. Author's Collection, ex-Imbert (1947).

Introduction

Numbers in the margin refer to the page where an illustration may be found

On entering a museum gallery containing Italian maiolica, the visitor who has never before seen – or consciously seen – this type of decorated pottery is likely to be struck by the splendour of the colours. Anyone entering a cathedral such as that at Chartres is also likely to be struck first by the colours of the stained glass windows. The next step in both cases will be to study the decoration to see what it is about.

The chief characteristic of Italian maiolica made during the Renaissance is undoubtedly the colouring – intense, pure and resonant with an inward glow that surpasses that of stained glass or the finest mosaics. This book is primarily concerned with the glazed and decorated pottery made in various parts of Italy over a period from, say, 1420 to 1565. This can be regarded as the classical period when the finest pieces were made. Many would say that – apart from a few simple earlier designs of great beauty and dignity – the best period was from 1470 to 1535. This is arguable, but all are agreed that in the long history of ceramics the Renaissance pottery we call maiolica was a brief glorious flowering of the genius of the earthenware-painters at a time when the spirit of man became truly conscious of itself and art attained new heights of dignity and beauty.

The word 'maiolica' has become a technical term implying that an earthenware dish, jug or other clay object has been coated after firing with a layer (usually white) containing tin oxide. This surface is ordinarily painted with some decoration and the piece, usually after being given an outer coating of glaze material, is then fired in the kiln for a second time. The second firing converts the pigments to the final colours as we see them, fuses these colours into the tin glaze and simultaneously melts the outer coating into a transparent glaze which serves the same purpose as varnish on an easel-painting. The tin-glaze process has been extensively used for a thousand years and is in use today and in many countries. It has largely replaced the simple process of coating the buff-coloured fired clay with white 'slip' (e.g. pipe-clay stirred up in water) and then painting on that.

The term 'maiolica' was originally applied to wares having a lustre (i.e. metallic sheen) decoration which traders of Majorca brought to Italy from Spain. During the 16th century the term came to be applied also to all the tin-glaze earthenware made in Italy itself, whether lustred or not.

The modelled ceramic wares of the Della Robbia family – e.g. Madonna and Child plaques in high relief – are sometimes classed as a branch of maiolica, but the subject is really a separate one and more appropriate to a discussion of sculpture. Little attention will be paid in this book to other ceramics (e.g. *sgraffiato* or scratched ware) made in Italy at the same time as but not having any of the characteristics of maiolica.

As with all artistic periods there were successive stages: a bold naive technically imperfect beginning, a maturity of grandeur, a commercialisation period with a deterioration of talent and inspiration, and finally a drift into decadence, which began, in the case of maiolica, about the middle of the 16th century. After this date new types of maiolica were produced – useful, decorative, often technically impressive, but lacking everything that makes the Renaissance an exciting period of artistic achievement having historical and – let us admit it – romantic associations.

The palette used by the maiolica-painters was limited to a few basic colours: blue, ochre, yellow, copper-green, 'manganese' (a brownish purple) and white. The ochre ranged from yellow to orange and brown, the latter sometimes being reddish. Other colours, including black, were obtained by mixtures. The materials that were used to give the required colours after firing in a kiln are discussed in the final section of the book (see page 54).

Having been first struck by the brilliant colours of maiolica, the spectator unfamiliar with this class of pottery will approach closely and examine the decoration on the various pieces. This brings us to the question of the subjects that interested the maiolica-painters and their customers. The form of decoration depends largely on the date, and on the centre where the maiolica piece was made. What we see may be a simple geometric, leafy or abstract design; alternatively, such a design may be combined with a simple illustration of a man, woman, animal or bird. Another type of decoration consists of a real picture which may

Rome (?). Bowl in manganese and blue showing the arms of Pope Calixtus III (Alfonso Borgia, 1455–1458). Diameter $8\frac{1}{4}$ in (21·0 cm). About 1455. Victoria and Albert Museum, London (VA 181).

Florence. Two-handled oak-leaf drugpot with dog on each side. Height 8 in (20·3 cm).
About 1435. Author's Collection, ex-Kolkhorst (1959), ex-E.L. Paget (1949), ex-Pringsheim
(1939), ex-G.J. de Osma. (Illustrated in Wallis, *Oakleaf Jars*, 1903, Fig. 33.)

occupy the centre or cover the whole plate including the rim,
or may be painted on a plaque. The subject may be a religious
one, e.g. **Abraham and Melchizedek, the Madonna of the
Girdle, the Virgin and Child** and **the Descent from the Cross**.
More usually the 'pictures' are of some story taken from classical
literature, e.g. **Aeneas escaping from Troy**, or **Metabus** (a city-
ruler of Italy) saving his little daughter Camilla from their enemies
by tying her to a spear which he throws across a river. Both

46, 48

23, 26

50, 49

these stories come from Virgil's *Aeneid*. It must be remembered that contemporary interest in the rediscovered authors of antiquity was immense, and nostalgia for the great days of Greece and Rome was reflected not only in literature, sculpture and painting, but in the so-called minor arts such as pottery.

Italy during the early Renaissance was full of painters, but the range of interest was very limited and confined mainly to religious subjects. The reason, no doubt, was that the churches were the chief patrons of the artists, although devotional pictures and portraits were bought by the upper classes. It is hardly necessary to say that the Renaissance painters could well have dealt with a far wider repertory of subjects if there had been a demand for them: we see the excellence of landscapes, still-lifes, flowers and animals introduced into the backgrounds of religious paintings.

It is interesting to recall that the austere Savonarola at the end of the 15th century wanted all 'profane' and pagan pictures to be destroyed, and there were bonfires in the streets of Florence. It would seem that the maiolica-painters and their customers took a delight in getting away from the religious paintings of their time and preferred historical and mythical themes or just decorative patterns or pictures of attractive women. Actual

Florence. Dish with bust of a woman.
Diameter $17\frac{1}{2}$ in (44·4 cm). About 1450.
Victoria and Albert Museum, London
(VA 73).

9

portraits of contemporary persons are practically never found, although there are many idealised and even caricatured pictures of men and women.

The newcomer to Italian maiolica, having studied the pleasing designs, may well wonder whether the maiolica dishes and jars were for decoration or use. Some of these pieces of painted earthenware, such as pharmacy jars, were obviously intended for use: the name of the medicament was often written in decorative Gothic letters on the pot. Such a jar (*albarello*) might be one of a group on the shelves of a domestic pharmacy. Although they were for use, many such **drugpots** are a delight to look at.

8, 15, 17, 25, 29, 30, 41

Decorated dishes might be used for fruit and no doubt were admired by guests who saw them laid out on a banqueting table. Isabella d'Este commissioned in about 1519 a complete **service of dishes** decorated with pictures of the story (*istoriato*) type with her coat of arms incorporated. Each dish was a superb work of art by the greatest maiolica painter of the time, Nicola Pellipario of Castel Durante and, from 1528 onwards, of Urbino.

It seems, in a way, sacrilege to use such dishes for food, but it also seems highly unlikely that such a service would be used solely for display. Small dishes (*tondini*) with deep wells were probably used for sweetmeats, nuts and the like. It has been

42

Faenza. Wall-tile in two shades of blue, ochre, yellow, green. 6 in $\times$ 12$\frac{1}{2}$ in (15·2 cm $\times$ 31·7 cm). About 1470–1480. Author's Collection.

11

suggested that they were also used as 'saucers' for small glasses. Elaborately painted wine coolers were obviously utilitarian objects, as were ceramic confinement sets which consisted basically of a bowl for broth, and a cover which served as a plate for bread; these were gifts to women who were expecting, or who had just had, a baby.

The point being made is that useful ceramic pieces were painted with all the skill that would be employed in producing a work of art intended for display. The possession of maiolica may have been an example of a status symbol; when presented as a gift it could be a form of propaganda for the city-state or for the ruler himself. Lorenzo il Magnifico of Florence wrote in 1490 to Roberto Malatesta, lord of Rimini, on receiving a gift of maiolica: 'They give me pleasure by their perfection and rareness, being novelties in these parts. They are valued more than if of silver, the donor's coat of arms reminding one constantly of their origin.' Today the equivalent of a superb maiolica dish might be a signed photograph of the sovereign.

Some jars and many dishes were clearly intended as ornaments. There are many gift plates with paintings of girls' heads and with a ribbon-like **label** giving the girl's name variously spelt, e.g. '**Aura**' (dated 1533), usually followed by the word 'Bella' or simply the letter 'B'. All recipients were automatically beautiful and occasionally divine. Sometimes the girl was described as both divine *and* beautiful. Such a dish, know as a *coppa d'amore* or *coppa amatoria*, would be given as a love-token. Most of these were made in Castel Durante. Some are extremely attractive, but they are in no sense portraits of the girl to whom such a plate might be given. A plate off-the-peg with her name on it would be given to a girl possessing that name, but many dishes of the portrait type (e.g. most of the large dishes painted in Deruta) have no names on them and are just more or less standardised but nonetheless attractive pictures of a woman or, more rarely, a man. It would be pure luck if the girl on any of these dishes looked even remotely like the loved one. They were probably betrothal or marriage gifts and would be treasured throughout life. The girls on the plates varied considerably; some, especially on **Deruta dishes**, have a grave beauty, reminiscent of Perugino's women, while others are disarmingly coy (VA 587). One *coppa d'amore* (VA 716) shows a gay-looking girl with the ribbon inscription: 'I will love whoever will love me.' One hesitates to speculate on the purchaser of such a plate.

Many large dishes made at Deruta have a couple of holes in the circular foot at the back. These holes were made before the pieces were fired. It is possible that such dishes, often of superb artistic quality, were brought into use on special occasions such as anniversaries, but it is clear that they were normally hung up as ornaments. The fact that the backs are usually coated only with a cheap transparent lead glaze may support the suggestion that the dishes were meant as decorations to be seen only from the front; it was certainly also an economy measure. The name 'show-plate' (*piatto da pompa*) is also significant. An easel-painting of a nuptial feast by Botticelli shows large decorative dishes arranged as ornaments, and there exists a maiolica plate illustrating a princely room with staggered shelves on which dishes are displayed. Some dishes belonging to a series—such as the triumphal procession plates marked with consecutive letters (e.g. VA 309 and one in the Fitzwilliam Museum)—were clearly intended to be displayed as a complete series round a room. Today it matters little whether a maiolica piece was originally used purely as a decoration or as a useful object.

Faenza. Portrait dish of a man. Diameter $14\frac{1}{2}$ in (36·8 cm). About 1470. Humphris Collection, ex-Bak sale.

Shapes and Types

The relationship between decoration and the shape of pottery has received much attention through the ages. There are many people, especially modern potters, who feel that the typical *istoriato* picture which covers the whole of a maiolica plate is an offence against the essential character of pottery. This is a very narrow view. A circle is one of the ideal shapes in which to paint a picture. Michelangelo (*Holy Family*), Botticelli, Domenico Ghirlandaio, Filippo Lippi and many others painted roundels. In pottery a flat disc or a rectangular slab was far more difficult to fire than a plate thrown on a wheel. Not only was it difficult to get a perfectly flat surface, but in the kiln a disc or plaque was very liable to warp. A plate with its depressed well and everted (turned-over) rim can be made accurately on a potter's wheel and it is–like a girder–a mechanically strong structure. The difference in level between the well and the rim produces a certain discontinuity, but *istoriato*-painters who often carried the picture right to the rim, such as **Pellipario** and **Guido Durantino**, took this in their stride. Many maiolica dishes–especially those made in Deruta–will satisfy all tastes because the pictorial portion is confined to the well, while round the flat rim is a **repeating pattern** of leaves, flowers or some other conventional scroll.

There is no logical reason for objecting to a painter's using a dish as he might use a canvas, a wood panel or a sheet of copper or glass. Painting on pottery using the maiolica technique has

46, 50

28, 30

14

many advantages. Although it is technically very difficult for reasons that will be given later, a great deal of satisfaction is obtained from the fact that today, after four or five hundred years, the paintings are as fresh as the day they came out of the kiln. When one considers the vicissitudes through which an easel-painting of the same period must have gone—the damage, the fading of colour, the loss of delicate glazes, the restoration—one appreciates the undisturbed perfection and resplendent colouring of a maiolica-painting sealed in for all time.

The various shapes of pieces of maiolica will be gathered from

Faenza. *Albarello* with a bird. Height $7\frac{1}{2}$ in (19·0 cm). About 1470–1480. Author's Collection, ex-Loeser sale (1960).

the examples illustrated. By far the greatest number of the products were either dishes, jugs or drugpots (alternatively called drugjars, pharmacy-jars or *albarelli*). The large number of drugpots is explained by the fact that well-to-do households had their own dispensaries. The dishes normally varied in diameter from 6 or 8 inches to 17 or 18 inches. Usually the dishes were much like modern dinner or soup plates, but intermediate-size plates, usually about 8 to 12 inches in diameter, were often shaped like large saucers and were provided with a short foot. The term *fruttiera* (fruit dish) or *tazza* was applied to these saucer dishes, and they were admirable for *istoriato*-paintings and 'portraits' as a large reasonably flat area was available. A smaller dish (*tondino*) was like a soup plate, but the rim was wide and the well comparatively deep and of small diameter; this shape is like an inverted cardinal's hat.

After the plate, the most popular shape is the cylindrical drugpot called in Italian *albarello*, a word probably derived from Arabic. The shapes of drugpots originated in Spain or the Middle East. It may be mentioned that Moorish physicians and chemists had a great reputation. In its commonest form the drugpot has no handles but is usually slightly waisted to facilitate lifting with one hand. The shape is not exhilarating, but the decoration very often is. Sometimes drugpots had lids, but usually the tops were covered with parchment secured by string tied round the groove near the top. Some drugpots had **two handles** which add to their attraction. As drugpots are usually seen from the front when on a pharmacy shelf, the main decoration is often only on one side. Pictures of the *istoriato* type are not very appropriate on a curved surface, so the decoration is usually a **portrait bust**, a coat of arms, **a bird**, an animal, e.g. **dog**, hare or lion, a medley of musical instruments or military arms, a cupid or a saint. This decoration is often combined with **scrolls of leaves and fruit** or abstract patterns.

Many pharmacy-jars have a **label with the name of the drug** painted in Gothic characters. This writing is always highly decorative which may have compensated for the drug's not being particularly remedial. The name of the medicament was usually

8, 17, 41

30,15,29,8

30

25

16

abbreviated as, indeed, it often is today on doctors' prescriptions.
15 The label on the back of the attractive **drugpot with a bird**
reads: 'loc sanū et exp', indicating that the content of the jar
was a cough mixture and expectorant. One typical medicament
was syrup of violets which does not sound particularly curative,
but its psychological value must have been considerable, as this
label is one of the most common. Another common product was
25 **electuary of roses.**

Liquid medicines were often kept in maiolica jugs with spouts
and a single handle. These teapot-like vessels were decorated in
much the same way as the cylindrical *albarelli.*

Some important plaques and discs have survived. In the Cluny
Museum in Paris is a magnificent Faenza disc with the Sacred
Monogram ('JES'—sometimes written 'IHS', but actually intend-

Faenza. Two-handled *albarello*. Height 10 in (25·4 cm). About 1470–1480. Alavoine Collection.

Faenza. *Albarello*. About 1470–1480. Alfred Spero Collection.

ed as the first three letters of the name 'Jesus'). It is dated 1475 and inscribed with the name 'Nicolaus de Ragnolis'; this foundation disc was embedded in a wall in Faenza. In the Victoria and Albert Museum there is a fine Faenza **plaque of the Madonna** 23 **and Child**, dated 1489, and another of the Entombment of Christ, 26 dated 1523 (VA 278). A **plaque of the Descent from the Cross** is also reproduced here. In the 18th century the Castelli potters produced a very large number of pictorial rectangular plaques, most of them painted with scenes from the Bible, the lives of the saints and the classical myths.

Other rather rare shapes are goblets, jugs, vases (some apparently purely decorative), pilgrim flasks of flattened globular shape, small pear-shaped jugs for holding consecrated oil, wine or water, small jugs similar to cream jugs, wine coolers, salt 19 cellars, **relief plaques** where the figures are moulded in the clay 55 and finally painted in colours, **free-standing bust-portraits**, inkstands with figures (e.g. the Nativity, VA 161 of about 1509) and finally – if, indeed, there is an end to what was made in maiolica – pieces that were almost toys, such as a model of a man playing an organ which was used as an inkstand (VA 852 of about 1555). Although modelling started at Faenza at the end of the 15th century (VA 158), a great deal of it took place around 1550 in Urbino.

In Castelli a brisk trade was carried on in the 18th century in moulded painted maiolica holy-water stoups. These incorporated complicated scenes in relief of the Virgin and Child, the Crucifixion, saints and angels. These must be regarded as utilitarian religious objects made on a commercial scale rather than works of art. Mention may be made in passing of votive offerings in the form of tablets depicting, for example, the Madonna in the sky and a sick or wounded person in the foreground.

Tiles with a tin-oxide enamel have been made throughout the history of maiolica. They may be classified as floor (pavement), wall and ceiling tiles. They are, in effect, small plaques which may take a variety of shapes and are usually painted with abstract decorative patterns, a portrait of a young man or woman, an animal, an inscription, a date, a coat of arms or emblem (*imprese*) or device of the owner of the palace or house. Sometimes a group of tiles forms an attractive overall pattern, but at other times the tiles are separate entities having no relationship with their neighbours. **A double wall-tile** has a brilliantly coloured decorative design characteristic of Faenza and datable to 1470–1480. The main colours are two shades of blue, with small quantities of lemon-yellow and of copper-green. The most famous floor tiles are those from the apartments of Isabella d'Este in the Castello Vecchio, Mantua. Maiolica tiles are sometimes found in the pavements of churches, e.g. San Petronio in Bologna (1487) and San Francesco in Deruta (1524); the latter pavement is now in the local museum. Another church pavement is in the Victoria and Albert Museum. These tiles often afford valuable evidence for determining the date and place of manufacture of other pieces of maiolica using similar designs, because one such tile may bear a date or there may be documentary evidence of when the pavement was laid down. Castelli in the 18th century made use of an assembly of tiles to produce a large picture cemented into a wall.

Faenza. Plaque with Annunciation in high relief. Height $19\frac{3}{4}$ in (50·2 cm). About 1475–1485. Humphris Collection, ex-Bak sale.

Centres of Manufacture

Anyone with experience of maiolica will ask himself where a particular piece was made. The centre of manufacture may be mentioned on the back of, say, a plate, e.g. 'in Urbino' (this appears on the back of the 1534 **Urbino plate**). But there are sometimes other sources of information. It is fairly safe to say that where wasters (kiln rejects) have been dug up there must have been a kiln. If during rebuilding or other excavations there is a preponderance of broken pieces with a particular type of decoration, it is persuasive that that category of pottery was made there. The coat of arms of a local family, if repeatedly found on excavated pots, may suggest local manufacture, although this is unreliable evidence. By making comparisons with pieces of definitely known origin it has been possible to build up a whole system of classification based on centres of manufacture. The sort of wares in which each centre specialised can be seen from the examples in this book since they have been grouped together.

It may well be asked why one should bother about where exactly a piece of Italian maiolica was made, but the desire to identify and classify places of origin is an extremely strong one. It also helps in dating a piece and may be the first step towards identifying the author. In England, 18th-century porcelain may be classed as Derby, Worcester, Chelsea or some other centre. Ceramics have even been categorised by different parts of a single city, e.g. Lambeth or Bow. Italian maiolica is classified by centres with far more reason. In spite of a common language,

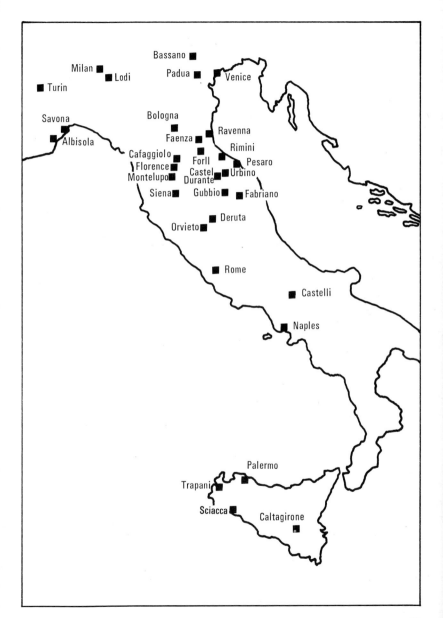

Bassano
Milan Lodi
Padua Venice
Turin
Savona
Bologna
Albisola Ravenna
Faenza Rimini
Cafaggiolo Forll Pesaro
Florence Castel Urbino
Montelupo Durante
Siena Gubbio Fabriano
Orvieto Deruta
Rome
Castelli
Naples
Palermo
Trapani
Sciacca Caltagirone

Italy was not really Italy as we know it until about a hundred years ago. The country was finally unified in 1870 when the papal states were annexed and Victor Emmanuel II became king of a united Italy.

During the period of classical maiolica the country was divided into city-states, vassal provinces, spheres of influence and the kingdom of Naples. These rival states led their own independent lives. Poor communications, wars and even banditry helped to isolate them and it is little wonder that individualistic maiolica centres grew up.

There were some thirty centres in Italy where maiolica was made, and these are shown on the map (page 21). Not more than

opposite Faenza. Dish with the arms of Matthias Corvinus, King of Hungary, and his second wife Beatrix, daughter of Ferdinand I of Aragon, King of Naples. Made between their marriage in 1476 and 1490. Diameter $18\frac{15}{16}$ in (48·0 cm). Metropolitan Museum of Art, New York (Fletcher Fund, 1946). (VA 150 and VA 151 belong to the same service.)

right Faenza. Fragment of a large dish showing lovers plighting their troth. Late 15th century. Diameter $4\frac{1}{2}$ in (11·5 cm). Rackham attributed this to Faenza. Author's Collection.

below Faenza. Plaque of the Virgin and Child. Height $18\frac{1}{2}$ in (47·0 cm). Dated 1489. Victoria and Albert Museum, London (VA 148).

fourteen were of importance during the classical period and of these the principal centres were Orvieto, Florence, Montelupo, Faenza, Deruta, Siena, Cafaggiolo and in the duchy of Urbino an important group consisting of Gubbio, Castel Durante, Urbino and Pesaro, these becoming prosperous from about 1516 onwards. Venice was a late starter around 1540 and became very active between 1550 and 1560. Montelupo had a second flowering in the 17th century with crude but not unattractive dishes having swashbuckling soldiers as their most usual decoration, while Castelli had a great commercial success around 1730 with somewhat pallid plaques and rather pretty plates. The Sicilian centres became active from early in the 17th century.

4   **Orvieto** was an early centre–perhaps the earliest–and is deservedly famous for its primitive and simple but striking designs in copper-green and manganese. These archaic pieces have, like much primitive work, a vigour–even a nobility–very much to our modern taste, but unhappily most of the few surviving pieces are badly damaged. The attribution to Orvieto of wares datable from 1300 or even earlier (most pieces were made between 1400 and 1450) is a matter more of convenience and courtesy than accuracy; such pieces were made in various places in the northern half of Italy and should be described as 'Orvieto-style'. Nevertheless, many of the extant examples have a rubbish-pit origin in Orvieto. Some have been subsequently 'restored' to a degree bordering on forgery.

     The next important centre of maiolica production in point of
8, 9   time was **Florence**. As kilns were not allowed in Florence itself because of the risk of fire, some suburb or perhaps Montelupo was the place where manufacture took place. The most famous
8   pots were the **two-handled oak-leaf jars** produced between 1425 and 1450. The decoration of these jars is in deep blue or a blue verging on black. The cobalt pigment is in impasto, and the designs of oak-leaves, faces, fleurs-de-lis, birds, dogs, etc. are outlined in manganese in which colour the oak-leaf stems are also painted. Around 1450 we get more sophisticated dishes (e.g. VA 73 and VA 74, which show the central well decorated with
9   **a woman's head** and a rabbit respectively); the illustrated dish

24

right Faenza. Plate with bust of a woman in contemporary costume. Diameter $9\frac{1}{4}$ in (23·5 cm). About 1505. Author's Collection, ex-Reitlinger (1954), ex-Pringsheim (1939).

below Faenza. *Albarello* (electuary of roses) in blue. Height $6\frac{1}{2}$ in (16·5 cm). About 1520–1530. Author's Collection.

above Faenza. *Coppa d'amore*: Lucrecia Bella. Diameter $10\frac{7}{16}$ in (26·5 cm). About 1525–1530. (A 296.) Humphris Collection.

Faenza. Plaque of the Descent from the Cross. 17 in × 12 in (43·2 cm × 30·5 cm). About 1520–1530. H.A. Cann Collection, ex-Bardini (illustrated in Bardini's catalogue in French and sold as Lot 88 at Christie's, 5th June 1899). From Marcantonio Raimondi's engraving (mentioned by Vasari) of Raphael's painting.

uses manganese, orange-yellow, green and blue. Between 1460 and 1470 we find *albarelli* painted with leaf-patterns in imitation of imported Manises (near Valencia) lustred wares. The colours are blue and manganese, the latter colour replacing the metallic lustre of the Spanish prototypes. As yet, lustre was not developed in Italy.

10–26 The greatest ceramics centre of all was **Faenza** which gave its name to *faience* and variants of this word in twenty-three countries from Spain to Russia, and from Finland to Japan. This small but noble city – Faventia in Roman times – may well have been producing post-primitive wares before Florence and is still a production centre with a school of ceramics and a famous museum, the International Museum of Ceramics in Faenza, which publishes an important journal *Faenza*. The Director of the Museum, Professor Giuseppe Liverani, has for long been a great authority on Italian maiolica.

Faenza was making primitive maiolica at least as early as Orvieto. By 1470 Faenza had gained the lead over Florence and was turning out a whole range of sophisticated wares, for example

15, 17 **drugpots of great distinction**. Before 1500 Faenza was producing plaques of complicated scenes. Between 1476 and 1490 a

22 **maiolica service** was made at Faenza for King Matthias Corvinus of Hungary and was never excelled later. This centre introduced *istoriato* dishes–pictures which told stories–an idea exploited later by Urbino. The roundel of 1475 in the Cluny Museum and the **tile** of about 1470–1480 have already been mentioned as examples of Faenza production. Faenza continued to make maiolica of special distinction until about 1530, but meanwhile other centres were growing up.

28–32 Around 1500 **Deruta** was active. A lustred and moulded wall-panel of St Sebastian in the Victoria and Albert Museum (VA437) is dated 1501. Deruta became especially famous for its lustred wares in which the decoration or parts of it were, by a special process, given a metallic sheen.

33, 35 **Gubbio** also became famous for its lustred wares. An unusually fine dish (hardly characteristic of this overrated centre)

33 in the Victoria and Albert Museum shows the **Three Graces**

27

Deruta. Large dish with lustre, showing profile of a girl. Diameter $14\frac{3}{16}$ in (36·0 cm). About 1510. Author's Collection, ex-Alavoine. (Compare VA 454, 455).

Deruta. Large lustred dish of the Incredulity of St Thomas. Diameter 16 in (40·6 cm). About 1515. Author's Collection, ex-Nicolier.

and is dated 1525. Gubbio was active from about 1505. Apart from its own manufactures which are uneven in quality, this centre applied its lustre process to painted pieces sent to it, especially from Urbino and Castel Durante. This lustre 'enrichment' is regarded by some (but not others) as an added attraction.

37   **Siena** had been a producer of Orvieto-style pottery in the 14th and 15th centuries but produced many excellent drugpots and dishes from 1500 onwards. A plate of distinction (VA 373) by Maestro Benedetto is dated 1510. The arms of the Piccolomini family of Siena (it provided two popes) are the only decoration

37   on **a large jug** of about 1500 which may be of local manufacture.

Deruta. *Albarello* with eagle. Height $9\frac{1}{2}$ in (24·1 cm). Early 16th century. Gambier-Parry Collection at the Courtauld Institute Galleries, London (Catalogue no. 28).

29

In 1506 Francesco de' Medici founded a private maiolica factory in his castle of **Cafaggiolo** near Florence. This produced many works of great beauty. A plate showing **a maiolica-painter at work** while interested visitors look on is an example.

Another important centre, **Castel Durante**, was obviously flourishing some time before the earliest date (1508) on a plate. When the present writer visited the pottery school in Urbania (the present name of Castel Durante) he was told that forty separate maiolica workshops were flourishing there in the first half of the 16th century. This fact should put a brake on too-facile attributions. The greatest son of Castel Durante was **Nicola Pellipario** who excelled at painting *istoriato* dishes. Undoubtedly his most important works were the seventeen plates (sometimes called **the Ridolphi service**) in the Correr Museum, Venice. The dishes were painted about 1515 and are remarkable for their overall bluish tonality, and a Faenza influence is possible. The colouring of these pieces is superb.

Deruta. Dish (not lustred) with a gallant and a lady. By Giacomo Mancini (El frate). Diameter 16 in (40·6 cm). About 1530–1545. Author's Collection, ex-Chevet.

Deruta. *Albarello* with bust of a woman in contemporary dress. Height 9 in (22·8 cm). About 1520–1525. (A 371.) Author's Collection.

Deruta. Two-handled polychrome baluster vase with emphasis on blue. Height $9\frac{7}{16}$ in (24·0 cm). About 1520. Alavoine Collection.

Deruta. Large dish (not lustred) with bust of a woman. Diameter $16\frac{3}{4}$ in (42·5 cm). About 1530. Museum für Kunst und Gewerbe, Hamburg (no. 18 of the 1960 catalogue).

46–57 **Urbino** became active about 1520, but the first known date on a piece of its maiolica is 1528. Urbino had a very great output until about 1550. Most of the wares were of the *istoriato* type and varied greatly in quality. In about 1550 this centre began to specialise in radically different pieces in which many small grotesques (spindly winged monsters, human bodies with leafy limbs, etc.) were painted on a white background.

The cities of Pesaro, Ravenna, Rimini, Forlì and Fabriano also produced some maiolica.

59, 60 **Venice**–oddly enough, considering its great reputation in painting–did not develop as a maiolica centre until about 1540, most of its output being manufactured between 1550 and 1570. The best work from Venice has been underrated, perhaps because of its late date, but many of its pieces are remarkable for the bold drawing, uncluttered design and sometimes its good colour. **The** 60 **Mercury and Minerva plate** is characteristic of run-of-the-mill Venice wares. Some of the pieces are rather poor imitations of earlier Urbino wares, but the blue pictorial dishes were highly

Gubbio. Dish with Three Graces. Diameter 12 in (30·5 cm). Signed by Maestro Giorgio (Andreoli) and dated 1525. Victoria and Albert Museum, London (VA 673).

59 original. The landscape of **the Lodovico plate** is datable between 1545 and 1550; a pure landscape without figures was at this period a great rarity in any kind of painting.

Sicily produced maiolica (mostly drugpots) in the period of decadence and after 1600. Trapani, Palermo, Siacca and Caltagirone were the principal centres. Some of the pieces are pastiches of much better examples made on the mainland some eighty years before, but there is a bold vigour and colouristic beauty in some of the wares (e.g. from Caltagirone and Trapani).

After the middle of the 16th century there was a move towards what one could call 'more-white' wares; a white background with sparse decoration began to be popular. Faenza led the way and, with its white pottery, changed the dinner tables of all Europe. Urbino, as we have seen, specialised in dishes decorated with a tiresome multitude of grotesques that would feel at home in a picture of hell by Bosch. There was also a fashion for three-dimensional objects such as inkwells; illustrated here is a **figure**
55 **of Christ** dated 1551.

33

Subjects, Dating and Authorship

The subject of a painting on, say, a maiolica dish is usually fairly obvious, especially if it is a religious one. Frequently – particularly after 1528 – the subject, whether religious or otherwise, is described on the back of the plate in contemporary Italian or Latin or a garbled combination of the two. The historical and mythical scenes are often easily identified but the painter sometimes helps one out by his inscription on the back; this will have been painted on before the outer glaze is applied. The inscription may include the date the plate was painted, the place where it was made and sometimes the signature of the painter. The handwriting of the inscription is itself often a clue to authorship. The better-known mythological subjects are easily recognised even if there is no explanatory description on the back of the plate. On the other hand, some pieces require a very detailed knowledge of the classics as no episode seems to have been too trivial to illustrate. A fruitful source was Ovid's *Metamorphoses*, and many maiolica plates were painted as adaptations of the primitive woodcuts that illustrated editions of the volume first printed in Venice in 1497. Virgil's *Aeneid* provided many incidents for the maiolica painters. Many other plates were copies or adaptations of engravings by Marcantonio Raimondi and others – especially of paintings by Raphael. (Certain maiolica was called 'Raffaele ware' and was once thought to be painted by Raphael.) The illustration of **the Three Graces** comes from an engraving of a painting based on an antique marble group in the Vatican.

33

34

Gubbio. Lustred plate with cupid. Diameter $9\frac{5}{8}$ in (24·5 cm). Signed by Maestro Giorgio (Andreoli) and dated 1528. Victoria and Albert Museum, London (VA 693).

Casa Pirota factory, Faenza.

Although marks are very common on later ceramics, there are very few on classical maiolica. Sometimes there are signatures, abbreviated signatures (such as 'F.R.') and a genuine mark such as a cross in a circle which indicated the Casa Pirota factory in Faenza.

50, 51 The dating of maiolica has been made relatively easy as a large number of pieces are actually **dated** – sometimes on the front of a plate but more usually on the back. There are other ways of dating, the most usual being stylistic comparison with actual dated wares. Sometimes an important event such as a marriage between noble houses affords a clue. Perhaps a plate is derived from an engraving the date of which is known; this will at least indicate that the plate is not earlier than the date of the engraving. A service made for a historical character such as Isabella d'Este may often be dated fairly closely. A coat of arms on a plate may also indicate approximately when a plate was made. For example, if a pope reigned for only two years a plate bearing his coat of

35

arms with the keys of Peter can be dated almost to the year.

The authorship of a piece of maiolica is sometimes as difficult to establish as in the case of an easel-painting. A score of maiolica painters are well known by name but of these only a few have a high reputation. Some are known by initials only, e.g. 'F.R.' or 'C.I.' (perhaps 'G.I.'). The greatest of all the painters, Nicola Pellipario, rarely signed his name: only four pieces with his signature are known – three with his monogram (a group of letters interlaced to form his forename Nicola or a slight variant) and one signed '**Nicola da V**' (the 'V' being an abbreviation of Urbino); the last is a plate in the British Museum. A much more prolific but less able artist who frequently dated and signed his name in full – or in an abbreviated form (sometimes only the letter 'X') – was **Francesco Xanto Avelli da Rovigo**. The names of most maiolica-painters, including some of very great skill, are unknown, but a few of the anonymous ones are so distinctive in style that they may be called by such names as 'the Master of the Resurrection panel'.

Some of the painters may have been potters and owned the '*botega*' (i.e. workshop – '*bottega*' in modern Italian) where their products were made. Others were painters only. On the backs of some plates are words which may be translated: 'made in the botega of Master Guido Durantino'. Nobody knows whether this Guido – son of Pellipario – was a painter himself or only the owner of the workshop. A Berlin Schlossmuseum dish of 1542 says it was made in the *botega* of Guido Vasaro (i.e. 'potter') da Castello Durante. Good paintings by the same hand are usually attributed to Guido himself, but the inscription referring to his *botega* does not in itself constitute an identification of a particular painter; in fact, a famous dish (dated 1528) in the Bargello in Florence bears the monogram of Nicola with the statement that it was made in the *botega* of Guido Durantino (his son) in Urbino. Doubts about authorship also apply to Giovanni Maria of Castel Durante whose name Zouan (Giovanni) Maria accompanied by the word *vasaro* (potter) appears on the back of a very fine dish (dated 1508) in New York with the coat of arms of Pope Julius II. Many excellent plates are clearly by this same hand or by the

Nicola
Pellipario
(see also 53)

53

49

Francesco
Xanto Avelli
da Rovigo

Francesco
Xanto Avelli
da Rovigo

36

Siena or Deruta. Large jug with
Piccolomini arms. Height $14\frac{1}{2}$ in
(36·8 cm). About 1500. Ex-Gondrexon
(1962), ex-Pringsheim (1939).

Orazio
Fontana

Virgiliotto
Calamelli
(Faenza)

hand of a close follower and are described as 'by' Giovanni Maria.

Xanto was clearly a painter (his signature is often followed by 'pinxit') and so was Nicola Pellipario.

The following are some of the better-known maiolica-painters and/or potters: Nicola Pellipario (sometimes called Nicola Fontana – a surname adopted later by the family of Nicola – or Nicola da Urbino), Guido Durantino (or Guido Fontana), Orazio Fontana (a son of Guido), Camillo Fontana (eldest son of Guido), Flaminio Fontana (younger son of Camillo), Giovanni Maria, Bergantini family, Francesco Xanto Avelli da Rovigo, Baldassare Manara, Guido Merlino (variously spelt), Francesco Durantino, Francesco Urbini, Pseudo-Pellipario (an invented name of a painter of Castel Durante), F.R. (and F.l.R.), Benedetto, C.I. (perhaps G.I.), Jacopo and the Fattorini family, Virgiliotto Calamelli, Giovanni Battista dalle Palle, Ferdinando Maria Campani, Domenigo da Venezia, Giorgio Andreoli (Maestro Giorgio), Ieronimo da Forlì, Jacomo da Pesaro, Maestro Lodovico, Francesco Mezzarisa (or Risino), Patanazzi family.

Siena. Drugpot with single handle. Height $8\frac{1}{2}$ in (21·6 cm). About 1510–1520. Bak sale.

38

The Spirit of the Renaissance

The historical and cultural associations of maiolica are of great importance and interest. A knowledge of the background will add to one's appreciation of what became at the end of the 15th century the finest painted pottery not only of Italy but of Europe. It is salutary to recall that in Britain in the 15th and 16th centuries it was usual to eat off wooden platters—or, in the case of the poor, off a thick slice of bread.

The maiolica we have been describing is as much part of the Renaissance as the sculpture of Donatello and Michelangelo and the paintings of Leonardo, Titian and Raphael. Collectors of Old Master Italian paintings should logically collect the pottery (often signed and dated) that went with those paintings in the palaces and houses of their country of origin.

The great variety of Italian maiolica is due to a multiplicity of factors, the two most important being firstly the conflict between religion and the humanistic revival and secondly the comparative isolation of the city-states.

Maiolica subjects may be divided into sacred and profane. Pious individuals (or those desiring to appear pious) would be glad to have maiolica dishes portraying scenes from the life of Christ or the Acts of the Apostles (e.g. the Conversion of St Paul). Strangely enough, Old Testament scenes were more popular than Christian ones. There has always been an especial interest in Old Testament incidents that seemed to be anticipations of later Christian events. A good example is the giving by Melchizedek—

the priest-king of Jerusalem – of bread and wine to Abraham after one of the latter's successful battles. This incident, described in Genesis XIV, 18, was interpreted as a forerunner of the Eucharist. A Christian mosaic showing the incident is in the nave of Santa Maria Maggiore in Rome and may be dated 432–440. The *loggie* of the Vatican were decorated by Raphael and his assistants with

46 **frescoes** showing Old Testament scenes, and the large **Abraham**
46 **and Melchizedek dish** is based on one of them. The superb
47 drawing of the figures can be clearly seen in the **detail** illustrated.

The Vatican fresco is the inspiration of the maiolica painting which, however, will be considered by many the more attractive design. This dish was described in a special article by Bernard

Cafaggiolo. Plate showing maiolica-painter at work. Attributed to Jacopo. Diameter $9\frac{1}{4}$ in (23·5 cm). About 1510–1515. Victoria and Albert Museum, London (VA 307).

Cafaggiolo. Inside of a bowl with the arms of a Medici pope. Diameter 14 in (35·6 cm). About 1520–1525. British Museum, London.

40

Rackham in *Keramik-Freunde der Schweiz*, No. 45 (January 1959) as 'beyond doubt' by Pellipario 'at the height of his powers'.

Swamping the religious subjects are the mythical and historical incidents. To this extent the pottery-painters were more in tune with the spirit of the times than the painters on canvas, wood or plaster. The Renaissance was an upsurge of humanistic feeling, a pride in man's place in this world rather than his place (or plight) in the next. The Italians had rediscovered – or felt they had re-discovered – the beauty, wisdom, dignity and morality of their Roman past. There was a great wave of admiration for the old classical writings of Rome and of Greece. Lorenzo il Magnifico of Florence is sometimes regarded as a great Medici patron of the

Cafaggiolo. Two-handled jar with pinecone ornament. Height $7\frac{3}{4}$ in (19·7 cm). About 1520–1525. Victoria and Albert Museum, London (VA 332).

arts—of painting and sculpture—but actually he was far more a patron of literature and poetry. Attitudes were changing. For a time Virgil overshadowed the Virgin, and poetry was more admired than piety. Italian culture was to be modelled on the pagan cultures of ancient Rome and Greece. The writings of Livy, Julius Caesar, Virgil (especially the *Aeneid*), Cicero, Ovid and Lucian (the Greek writer) were treated with as much reverence—and more interest—than the Bible. The study of Roman ruins and the excavation of statues and other remains aroused great enthusiasm. The printing of books such as Ovid's *Metamorphoses* (in Venice in 1497), complete with naive woodcuts to illustrate the stories, stimulated the widespread interest in the Roman heritage.

All this is reflected in the maiolica paintings. Guido Durantino in the large dish dated 1535 has illustrated with fidelity the story 50 of **Aeneas leaving burning Troy**, taking his father Anchises on his back and his son Ascanius by the hand. The details correspond very closely with Virgil's account (*Aeneid*, Book 2, line 700 onwards). In this dish, incidentally, one can see how characters

Castel Durante. Plate with Orpheus. Diameter $10\frac{5}{8}$ in (27·0 cm). About 1515. One of 17 plates by Nicola Pellipario in Correr Museum, Venice.

Castel Durante. Plate with story of Phaedra and Hippolytus. Centre is decorated with the coat of arms of Isabella d'Este. Painted by Nicola Pellipario. Diameter $10\frac{3}{4}$ in (27·15 cm). About 1519. Victoria and Albert Museum, London (VA 547).

are shown more than once in different stages of the story—a common practice of maiolica-painters and, indeed, of artists since the time of the ancient Egyptians.

Ovid's mythical stories provided scores of subjects, and as woodcuts were available the maiolica-painters had something to go on, although it was customary to vary the picture. The engravers were also using classical themes, and the maiolica-painters often copied engravings or selected parts of them. Slavish copying was very rarely resorted to, and normally the maiolica-painters used their imagination, often with happy results. In the popular pagan revival no piece of pottery was safe from the desire to paint on it some scene from classical literature. This, of course, could not go on, and after about the middle of the 16th century there was a collapse of interest in ceramic pictorialism which, however, flickered on into decadence—the ultimate fate of all art-forms.

The historical background played as big a part as the spirit of the Renaissance in maiolica production. In the Italy of the 15th and 16th centuries the two greatest figures were the Emperor, the head of the Holy Roman Empire, and the pope with his papal states. The Emperor Charles V was based in Germany but was in full control of Spain (his son Philip II became ruler of that country and the Netherlands) and was the overlord of much of Italy. The Emperor created nobles—usually in return for money or military assistance—and from time to time intervened in the politics of the Italian states. Italy was subject to invasion from France and Spain. The pope, based on Rome, was not only the religious head of Christendom but also a temporal ruler of great tracts of Italy. He is today the ruler of the tiny state of Vatican City, but during the Renaissance he was almost continually involved in political intrigue, the making and breaking of alliances, and in wars of defence or territorial aggrandisement. Even in city-states there might well be parties which supported either the pope (Guelphs) or the Emperor (Ghibellines).

South of Rome was the King of Naples and in the north the powerful Duke of Milan—the latter either uncomfortably or conveniently close to France. In 1492 Charles VIII of France, in pursuit of a claim to the throne of Naples, invaded Italy. In 1510

we find the pope (Julius II), with France and the Emperor as allies, warring against Venice, and in 1527 a mixed Spanish and German army sacked Rome, Pope Clement VII – Giulio de' Medici – becoming a prisoner in his castle of Sant' Angelo.

The pope in those times was likely to be a member of one of the ruling families of Italy: Julius II was a Della Rovere, the ducal family of Urbino, while Leo X (1513–1521) and Clement VII (1523–1534) were members of the Medici family of Florence. Or he might be a Spaniard: Pope Alexander VI (1492–1503) was Roderigo Borgia. The very name 'Borgia' conjures up a picture of corruption, lust, cunning, assassination and military adventure. Alexander's son Cesare Borgia (who, incidentally, ruled Deruta for a time) was made a cardinal at seventeen by his father. He resigned to become an able but unscrupulous captain-general bent on enlarging the papal territories. He conquered Urbino in 1502. The pope's fifth child Lucrezia Borgia became a pawn in the power game of the period, marrying as her fourth husband Alfonso d'Este who became Duke of Ferrara in 1505. She thus became a relation by marriage of Isabella d'Este.

The various states which made up Italy during the 15th and 16th centuries were not only of widely different sizes but had different constitutions. Venice was a republic with a doge as an elected president – a system that continued until the end of the 18th century. Florence was the intellectual centre of Italy, the very heart of the Renaissance movement in literature, archaeolo-

Castel Durante. Plate with nude woman in the centre, rim decorated with trophies (musical instruments, scores and mock-Hebrew inscriptions). Diameter 11 in (28 cm). About 1525. (A 401, where Rackham attributes it to Pellipario.) Humphris Collection.

Castel Durante. Dish with portrait of a warrior labelled 'PALLAMEDE'. By Pellipario. Diameter $8\frac{5}{8}$ in (22·0 cm). About 1525. (A 398.) Humphris Collection.

Castel Durante. *Coppa d'amore* with bust of a girl and label 'AVERA B'. Diameter 9 in (22·8 cm). Dated 1533. Author's Collection.

gical research and the arts, particularly painting and sculpture. It was a republic, and its citizens were very conscious of their rights, but certain families wielded excessive power. Of these families the Medici maintained a supremacy for many years, partly because they were rich merchants and bankers and partly because in their earlier years they had supported the common people against the noble families. (The three-balls sign of a pawn-broker's shop derived from the six balls of the Medici arms.)

The Dominican prior Savonarola (1452–1498) acquired a great reputation in Florence as a religious reformer and prophet. In 1494 he led a revolt which expelled the Medici. He denounced the Borgia Pope Alexander VI and in 1498 was tortured, hanged and burnt for heresy. Two Medici popes of special interest to students of maiolica are Leo X (seen in a procession in VA 318) who sparked off the Reformation by selling indulgences, and Clement VII who refused to invalidate Henry VIII's marriage to Catherine of Aragon and denounced his marriage to Anne Boleyn. Incidents in the lives of the popes appear on maiolica, as do their coats of arms which consist of the crossed keys of Peter, the tiara and the family coat of arms. A **Cafaggiolo bowl** shows a Medici pope's coat of arms. On the outside of this bowl are his arms and those of families related to him: Strozzi, Orsini and Salviati.

Florence ceased to be a republic when the Emperor Charles V in 1534 created Alessandro de' Medici hereditary Duke of Tuscany with Florence as his capital.

left Raphael. *Abraham and Melchizedek*. Fresco in *Loggie*, Vatican.

Many of the smaller city-states, such as Urbino, Pesaro and Rimini, were at various times virtually petty kingdoms ruled by tyrants (in the Greek sense) with absolute power which might be restricted to a certain extent by being subject to some overlord or powerful ally. These dukedoms, marquisates and lordships were hereditary, but such dynasties might change as a result of failure of an heir, marriage, war, political pressure short of war, popular uprisings or mutiny by an army leader. Such a military leader was the bastard Federigo di Montefeltro who seized power from his brother in Urbino in 1444, governed wisely, encouraged the arts and built the palace that stands there today.

The maiolica-painters sometimes depict directly or indirectly the interests, conflicts and social patterns of their times. One could make a selection of maiolica pieces that reflected the social life, the ducal grandeurs and the historical events. Examining such pieces in their right order would be like turning the pages

left Urbino. Large dish with Melchizedek, priest-king of Jerusalem, giving Abraham bread and wine. Based on the Raphael painting (see 46 top). Diameter $16\frac{1}{2}$ in (42·0 cm). About 1528. (Compare the signed Pellipario dish of 1528 in the Bargello, Florence.) In an article on this dish in *Keramik-Freunde der Schweiz*, No. 45 (January 1959), p. 21, Bernard Rackham declares it to be 'beyond doubt' by Nicola Pellipario 'when at the height of his powers'. Author's Collection, ex-Nicolier, ex-Baronne de Ravignan (Hôtel Drouot, 3rd December 1942, Lot 44), ex-Paul Mame of Tours (Georges Petit, 26th April 1904, Lot 198).

Detail of the Abraham and Melchizedek dish (see 46 bottom), showing the quality of the drawing.

of history, and some knowledge of the period adds greatly to the intellectual pleasure of looking at maiolica.

It was quite customary for a noble or prelate to order maiolica pieces on which would appear his coat of arms either by itself or more frequently as an addition to the painting. The Victoria and Albert Museum has **an early bowl** painted in purple and dark blue with the arms of the Borgia pope Calixtus III (1455–1458); this piece was found on the bed of the Tiber and is therefore not in pristine condition. The arms incorporate the bull of the Spanish Borgia family, the crossed keys of St Peter drawn in a formalised rather than a realistic way, and the papal tiara. There are many pieces with the arms of the Medici (the family, incidentally, provided four popes), Piccolomini, Colonna, Della Rovere, Este, Malatesta, Montefeltro, Orsini, Petrucci, Pitti, Pucci, Ridolfi, Salviati, Visconti, Strozzi and other historically important families who produced popes, famous generals, dukes, cardinals, assassins and courtesans–a list that sounds like a roll-call of the famous and infamous.

In the Victoria and Albert Museum alone, some 150 different coats of arms appear on maiolica. Sometimes the coat of arms of a city, e.g. the fleur-de-lis of Florence (VA 39), appears on a jar or dish. Towards the end of the 16th century Venetian potters were

Urbino. Plate with the Madonna, after her Assumption, lowering her girdle to St Thomas. No inscription. By Xanto. Diameter 11 in (27·9 cm). About 1528. Mentioned by Rackham in *Faenza* XLIII, 1957, p. 99, and by Joan Prentice von Erdberg in *Burlington Magazine* CIII, 1961, p. 299. Figures are from an engraving of Baldovinetti's lunette in San Niccolò, Florence. Author's Collection, ex-Whittall (1947).

48

sedulously turning out pieces with coats of arms of petty merchants and brewers of southern Germany.

The purposes of coats of arms were manifold. It was a way of marking one's property. The main reason, however, for painting them on maiolica was self-assurance and self-advertisement. As we have seen, the popes were just as actuated by family pride as the nobles. Such pieces were often given to personal or political friends. Clearly, the more beautiful and noble-looking the jar or dish, the more the recipient would be impressed. Sometimes the joint coats of arms of bride and bridegroom would be painted on a service or individual pieces to celebrate a marriage. The piece would then become a decorative and – with care – an imperishable form of marriage-lines.

Needless to say, coats of arms – especially when they incorporate the arms of husband and wife (as in the case of King Matthias Corvinus of Hungary and his second wife Beatrix, daughter of Ferdinand I of Aragon, King of Naples) are a means of dating a piece of maiolica. **The Faenza dish** with their arms must be dated between 1476 when the couple were married and 1490 when King Matthias died. Matthias was the greatest of his country's kings, a worthy son of a father who held up the Turkish invasion of Europe at Belgrade in 1456.

22

Urbino. Plate (lustred at Gubbio) showing Metabus throwing his spear – with his daughter Camilla bound to it – across a river. Diameter $10\frac{1}{4}$ in (26·0 cm). Signed by Xanto and dated 1534. H.A. Cann Collection.

Urbino. Dish showing Aeneas escaping from burning Troy with his father Anchises and son Ascanius; in a second scene he is ritually washing his hands in a stream outside Troy before touching household gods held by Anchises. Scene from *Aeneid*, Bk 2, line 700 onwards. By Guido Durantino. Diameter $17\frac{1}{2}$ in (44·4 cm). Dated 1535. Author's Collection, ex-Deutsch (1963), ex-Clarence Mackay, ex-Lord Duveen (1916), ex-Baron Maurice de Rothschild, ex-Baron Adolphe de Rothschild who formed the collection, 1870–1890.

A piece of maiolica bearing a coat of arms is of historical and chronological interest but also, to us, of sentimental value. There is a feeling that the particular piece will certainly have been ordered, probably owned and possibly handled by the person whose coat of arms it bears. The blazonry is often a thing of beauty in itself, and there is evidence that some maiolica painters (such as Baldassare Manara of Faenza) invented spurious coats of arms to make their plates more attractive and to impress a customer.

42 Two of the most famous services are those of **Isabella d'Este** and Anne de Montmorency (VA 626, dated 1535) who–despite a deceptive Christian name–was Grand-maître and later Constable of France. Isabella d'Este, daughter of Ercole I of Ferrara, married in 1490 Gianfrancesco Gonzaga, Marquis of Mantua who died in 1519. She was a woman of intellect and culture and a patron of the arts. On the death of her husband she commissioned

42 –as we have seen–**a service** to be painted by Nicola Pellipario. A plate from this service is in the Victoria and Albert Museum. The coat of arms is Isabella's and shows the Gonzaga arms impal-

Back of the Aeneas dish (see 50) showing the date '1535'.

ing those of Este. For good measure, there were added Isabella's stoic motto *Nec spe nec metu* ('Without hope or fear') and her personal devices: the figure 'XXVII' and a scroll of music. The figure twenty-seven is thought to be a play upon the words '*vinte*' (overcome) and '*sette*' (seven), referring to seven intrigues against her husband which she claimed to have defeated. Another device representing a more feminine source of satisfaction is the sheet of music with bars and notation. This refers to the sensation caused when Isabella d'Este appeared in a garment decorated with a scroll of music at fêtes given in 1502 in honour of Lucrezia Borgia. It appears that Isabella stole the show.

This plate is an example of the great painter's obtaining his inspiration from a crude woodcut in Ovid's *Metamorphoses* published in Venice by Lucantonio Giunta in 1497.

The Montmorency service has on each piece the Grand-maître's coat of arms on a shield hanging from a tree. On the back of the plate (VA 626) is the inscription: 'fabula d Ipolito e Phedra–In Botega de M⁰ Guido durantino in Urbino 1535' ('legend of Hippolytus and Phaedra–In the workshop of Master Guido Durantino at Urbino 1535').

The arbitrary power exercised by the heads of the various states in Italy did not prevent these rulers from sharing in the general interest in Renaissance ideas. In fact, they were often scholars and general patrons of the arts. The maiolica factory of Cafaggiolo near Florence was initiated by a Medici in 1506. The Sforza of Milan, the Gonzaga of Mantua, the Montefeltro and later the Della Rovere of Urbino, the Este family of Ferrara and the popes in Rome all had a profound respect for the arts. As regards maiolica in particular, the Dukes of Urbino were obviously supporters of the local potteries and those in other parts of the duchy, e.g. in Castel Durante. In Faenza its lord Galeotto Manfredi was a patron and the many dishes and drugpots with a peacock-feather design are regarded as a subtle compliment to his mistress Cassandra Pavona of Ferrara (for whom he lost his life in 1488), '*pavo*' being the Latin for peacock. In fact, all the centres of maiolica manufacture regarded the art as good for prestige, good for interstate relations and good for business.

Urbino. Plate with a sacrifice to
Diana. By Nicola Pellipario. Diameter
$10\frac{1}{4}$ in (26·0 cm). About 1530–1540.
British Museum, London.

Back of the Diana plate (see above)
showing signature 'Nicola da V'.
(See also 36.)

Method of Manufacture

The technique of maiolica potting and painting requires some further explanation because it needed a very special skill that affected the overall result. The following details necessarily repeat some of the information given earlier.

The essential characteristic of maiolica is that the main clay 'body', after firing in a kiln, is coated with a thin white layer of a mixture containing tin oxide. The resultant white matt surface is ideal for painting on. The tin used in making the tin oxide was usually obtained from Cornwall via Flanders and was unjustly called 'Flanders tin'. The Spanish wares imported into Italy were decorated with lustre paint which on a special firing left a metallic sheen where the lustre paint had been applied. The early Florentine products tended to imitate the Spanish motifs, but no immediate attempt was made to copy the lustre technique. In fact, this became a later technical development in which the cities of Deruta and Gubbio specialised. Instead of lustre, the Italian potteries normally used non-lustrous paints applied to the white stanniferous (i.e. tin-containing) surface layer, the dish or other ceramic object being then fired a second time.

The process of making, say, a maiolica plate was as follows. The plate would be formed from refined clay on a potter's wheel and allowed to dry out to a leathery consistency. It would then be baked in a kiln heated by burning wood. The baked clay is now brownish buff or reddish in colour and the material is called the 'biscuit' or 'body' which is relatively soft and may easily be

Urbino. Bust of Christ. Height $5\frac{1}{2}$ in (13·9 cm). Dated 1551. Author's Collection, ex-E.L. Paget (1949), ex-Marcioni & Lucatelli sale (1914).

scratched. It rather resembles a flowerpot in colour and strength. A sort of whitewash of milky consistency and called 'bianco' is now prepared; this contains a powdered mixture of tin oxide, lead oxide and marzacotto which is a potassium silicate made by fusing a mixture of sand and calcined wine-lees—the scrapings from inside empty wine-casks. (Instead of wine-lees the ashes of certain burnt plants were sometimes used.) This marzacotto provides the 'glassy' element. The plate is usually completely immersed in this 'whitewash' (which is really the finely powdered ingredients held in suspension in water) and withdrawn at once. The plate is now allowed to dry. The smooth white surface will be matt and absorbent like blotting-paper. It is called the 'tin enamel' or 'tin glaze', and pottery with this surface is often called tin-glazed earthenware. (The tin-oxide glaze remains white after firing, whereas lead glaze becomes transparent.) The maiolica-painter now paints his design on the surface. His paints are unlike those of the ordinary painter because they are earth materials and metal oxides whose colours are only brought out when the plate is fired for the second time. Fine paintbrushes were used, the whiskers of mice being particularly popular.

A person looking at the finished painting before firing would probably not have a satisfactory idea of the subject. Not only has the artist to know the colours as they will appear after firing, but he cannot afford to make mistakes because he cannot repaint the faulty passage. It is rather as though he had painted with water-colours on white blotting-paper. The good painter must therefore be assured and skilled.

Before the plate is put in the kiln for its second and final firing, the paint is allowed to dry; the plate is then dipped in a second bath of milky liquid which coats the painted plate with materials which will later fuse in the kiln and produce a transparent glaze (i.e. a glass coating) over the plate. This final glaze was known as 'coperta' and was a lead glaze consisting of powdered marzacotto and lead oxide, the mixture being stirred up in water. This 'varnish' glaze was not used on early pieces.

When the coperta has dried, the plate is given its second firing in the kiln. The pigments of the painting are turned to their

Urbino. Dish with central figure of St Thomas (patron saint of carpenters) surrounded by Raphael-type grotesques. Diameter $10\frac{3}{4}$ in (27·3 cm). About 1555. Humphris Collection, ex-Bak sale.

desired colour by the heat and are fused and fixed in the tin-oxide enamel coating. The external coating simultaneously melts and provides a transparent glass-like covering for the painting. This external lead glaze–it is virtually glass melted over the decoration–protects the painting and also renders the colours more brilliant. A similar improvement of colour is obtained by varnishing an oil painting.

57

The important merit of the tin-oxide coating (the enamel) is that it imprisons the colours so that there is no smudging of outlines or dissolving (running) of colours into the outer transparent glaze. The luminosity of all but completely opaque colours is enhanced by the white backing provided by the tin-oxide layer next to the biscuit.

A rare but interesting technique was sometimes used (VA 495) to obtain flesh-tints. Faces and hands—in fact, any bare-flesh areas—on the tin-oxide layer were scraped away so that by abrasion the white layer was removed leaving the buff biscuit to represent flesh. Another painting technique was to use a sharply pointed wooden tool to incise patterns in, say, an area of blue. The incision only goes down to the white tin-oxide layer and not through it. Delicate white patterns are thus easily made on a blue background.

A very different process is that used in the case of what is usually called *sgraffiato* or *sgraffito* (i.e. scratched) ware which was made in quantity in the 15th and 16th centuries at Bologna and other parts of northern Italy. A tin-oxide base was not used; instead, the biscuit was coated with white or light-coloured slip—a clay-and-water mixture (pipeclay was often used) that dried on the biscuit. A pattern such as a human figure or leafy scroll is 'drawn' on the slip by a pointed metal or wooden tool that cuts through the white slip down to the buff or reddish biscuit. Instead of mere scratched lines, substantial areas of slip are sometimes cut away to give a dark buff background to figures or other white areas of decoration. Sometimes the incised lines or cutaway parts are filled in with colour, and the whole plate is then dipped in a lead glaze and refired. The transparent lead glaze is usually somewhat yellowish as a result of iron impurities in the lead oxide. Sometimes the lead glaze is deliberately tinted, e.g. with brown, green or purple pigment. Although the incised drawing is often very satisfying, the colours (if used) fuse into the external lead glaze which tends to run and carry with it some of the colours. The result is usually an unhappy blurring of the colouring and a confusing of the picture incised on the plate. The clay was sometimes moulded to produce relief effects or complete

Venice. Plate showing a
romantic seascape with a
castle on a cliff, in blue.
Maestro Lodovico workshop.
Diameter $7\frac{5}{16}$ in (18·5 cm).
About 1540–1550. (A 462.)
Author's Collection.

free-standing three-dimensional figures (the St George of VA 1376). Some early authors called *sgraffiato* ware 'mezza-maiolica', but the term has been indiscriminately used and has caused such confusion that it is best forgotten.

Venice. Plate of Mercury and Minerva. Workshop of Domenigo da Venezia. Diameter $9\frac{1}{2}$ in (23·0 cm). About 1560. Private collection.

The materials used as pigments for decorating maiolica must be capable of standing up to the high temperatures required to fuse the tin enamel on which the pattern or picture is painted. The raw materials are usually metallic oxides which undergo colour changes on firing, as has already been explained. The pigments that were commonly used were:

Green: derived from copper. This is a bluey-green.

Blue: usually derived from cobalt.

Yellow: derived from antimony.

Orange and brown: derived from iron rust.

Purple: derived from manganese.

Black and dark brown: derived from a mixture of pigments.

White: derived from tin oxide.

Red: a really satisfactory red does not appear on classical maiolica. A reddish brown appears on Cafaggiolo pieces and tends to rise above the level of the surrounding area (impasto). It is also commonly found on Siena pieces, but rarely on the wares of other centres. Armenian bole was sometimes used.

The earliest pieces used only one or two colours. Copper-green outlined by manganese decorated many Orvieto pieces. Florentine pieces of the second quarter of the 15th century (such as oak-leaf drugpots) used cobalt blue with outlines and branches in manganese purple. Orange-yellow came next and by 1470 all the chief colours are found. A fine lemon-yellow appears on some **Faenza pieces** of about 1470. Blue remained for a long time the favourite colour of Faenza, whereas in the second quarter of the 16th century Urbino became the chief factory of maiolica and specialised in the production of wares in which shades of ochre, orange and yellow predominated.

As regards the application of lustre pigments, two raw materials are used in the paint mixture—oxide of silver and oxide of copper. The silver produces a pale brassy lustre while the copper gives a rich ruby colour. Appropriate mixtures of silver and copper gave intermediate colours. In **dishes made at Deruta** the combination of an ochre lustre and blue can be seen in superbly drawn dishes. Gubbio became famous for both its brassy and ruby lustre which latter, however, was also used sometimes

61

in the early Deruta wares. The silver or copper oxide paints were applied to the dishes after the second firing. The dish was then fired at a relatively low temperature and black smoke allowed into the kiln. The carbon of the smoke combined with the oxygen of the oxide leaving a metal film which was then wiped to clean it.

35 Not only did Gubbio produce **its own maiolica incorporating**
49 **its lustre**, but painted pieces from Castel Durante and **Urbino** were often sent to Giorgio Andreoli of Gubbio to be 'enriched' by the addition of lustre. This lustre might be applied to blank spaces (e.g. the sun and/or its rays might be painted in) or the lustre might be painted over 'ordinary' painted areas. This latter process often spoilt the richness of the colour without any observable compensating advantage. The backs of most lustred pieces were decorated with rough leafy scrolls in lustre and were sometimes signed and dated by the lustre expert Maestro Giorgio. The pottery-painter Piccolpasso wrote in the middle of the 16th century that 94 per cent of wares sent for lustre enrichment became failures. This figure seems unlikely, but the process was certainly a risky one. It may be mentioned that many maiolica pieces have been wrongly credited to Gubbio when the main painting was carried out elsewhere and only the lustre applied at Gubbio. Maestro Giorgio showed by his many signatures that he had a stronger publicity sense than some of the painters at

Maestro
Giorgio of
Gubbio

Italian. Large dish with
Devotion of Marcus Curtius.
Diameter $19\frac{1}{4}$ in (48·9 cm). Dated 1556.
A. Spero Collection, ex-Earl of Chesterfield.

Urbino and Castel Durante whose products he – and later his sons – enriched or ruined.

This short account of the manufacturing processes will have sufficed to show that the final results were achieved by surmounting one obstacle after another. When a highly skilled and imaginative maiolica-painter cooperated with a potter of ability the resultant maiolica could become a thing of the rarest beauty.

W.B. Honey – an authority of wide ceramic tastes – once wrote that maiolica provided 'decoration more splendid and delicate in colour and bolder and more sensitive in drawing than anything done on pottery before or since . . . For the actual beauty of its decoration it has always been praised and for this it is admired and collected today.'

Acknowledgements

Photographs were kindly provided by the author and the following: Alavoine Collection; British Museum, London; H.A. Cann Collection; Correr Museum, Venice; Courtauld Institute of Art, London University; Cyril Humphris Ltd; Mansell Collection, London; Metropolitan Museum of Art, New York; Museum für Kunst und Gewerbe, Hamburg; Sotheby & Co.; Alfred Spero Collection; Victoria and Albert Museum, London.

COUNTRY LIFE COLLECTORS' GUIDES

Series editor Hugh Newbury
Series designer Ian Muggeridge

Published for Country Life Books by
THE HAMLYN PUBLISHING GROUP LIMITED
LONDON · NEW YORK · SYDNEY · TORONTO
Hamlyn House, Feltham, Middlesex, England

ITALIAN MAIOLICA
ISBN 600431843
© The Hamlyn Publishing Group Limited 1972
Printed in Great Britain by Butler & Tanner Limited, Frome and London